LOUIS PASTEUR

Essential Lives

LOUIS

PASTEUR

GROUNDBREAKING CHEMIST & BIOLOGIST

by Sue Vander Hook

Content Consultant:
Becky Seabrook, vice president, Education
John P. McGovern Museum of Health & Medical Sciences

ABDO
Publishing Company

CREDITS

Published by ABDO Publishing Company, 8000 West 78th Street, Edina, Minnesota 55439. Copyright © 2011 by Abdo Consulting Group, Inc. International copyrights reserved in all countries. No part of this book may be reproduced in any form without written permission from the publisher. The Essential Library™ is a trademark and logo of ABDO Publishing Company.

Printed in the United States of America,
North Mankato, Minnesota
112010
012011

 THIS BOOK CONTAINS AT LEAST 10% RECYCLED MATERIALS.

Editor: Paula Lewis
Copy Editor: David Johnstone
Interior Design and Production: Kazuko Collins
Cover Design: Kazuko Collins

Library of Congress Cataloging-in-Publication Data
Vander Hook, Sue, 1949-
  Louis Pasteur : groundbreaking chemist & biologist / by Sue Vander Hook.
    p. cm. -- (Essential lives)
  Includes bibliographical references.
  ISBN 978-1-61714-783-8
  1. Pasteur, Louis, 1822-1895--Juvenile literature. 2. Scientists --France--Biography--Juvenile literature. 3. Microbiologists-- France--Biography--Juvenile literature. I. Title.
  Q143.P2V57 2011
  509.2--dc22
  [B]

                        2010041186

TABLE OF CONTENTS

Chapter 1

Louis Pasteur in his laboratory

ONE OF THE GREATEST

On October 17, 1885, 62-year-old scientist Louis Pasteur received an urgent letter. It was from Pierre-Joseph Perrot, mayor of Villers-Farlay, a small village in eastern France. Mayor Perrot explained that Jean-Baptiste Jupille, a 15-year-old shepherd boy, had been attacked by a dog with rabies. The teenager and five younger shepherds had been tending their sheep in a meadow when the crazed, rabid dog appeared.

The young boy fought off the dog and eventually killed it with his shoe. He saved his companions, but he was severely bitten on his hands. The boy's life was now in grave danger. Rabies was transmitted through saliva, and it was almost always fatal.

Colleague

The French physician and scientist Pierre-Paul-Émile Roux (1853–1933) was one of Pasteur's closest colleagues. In his research, Roux discovered the first effective treatment for diphtheria. He also worked on vaccines for tetanus, tuberculosis, syphilis, and pneumonia.

First Rabies Vaccine

It had been four years since Pasteur and his colleague, Pierre-Paul-Émile Roux, had developed the first rabies vaccine. In 1881, Roux had removed the diseased spinal cord from a rabbit that had died of rabies. The spinal cord was left to dry for two weeks, which weakened the rabies virus so that it would not cause an active infection. Pasteur then injected the weakened virus into 50 healthy dogs. The dogs became slightly ill but eventually recovered. More importantly, their immune systems—their bodies' natural defense system against disease—had been strengthened against the rabies virus. When injected again with a strong dose of rabies, the dogs did not become sick. Pasteur reported that the vaccine had made "fifty dogs of all ages and all races immune to rabies without a single failure."[1]

Pasteur also found that dogs could be vaccinated and saved after they were bitten by a rabid animal. It took several weeks for rabies symptoms to appear. If the dogs were injected with the vaccine soon

What Is Rabies?

Rabies is caused by a virus that leads to severe inflammation of the brain. The disease is usually spread through the bite of an infected warm-blooded mammal, most commonly a dog or a bat. Rabies is nearly always fatal unless treated before severe symptoms set in.

Once a person is bitten, the virus is dormant for several weeks before traveling to the brain through the nerves. Victims suffer from headaches and fever, vomiting, a sore throat, and muscle pain. They also experience spasms, seizures, hallucinations, confusion, depression, and sensitivity to light, sound, and touch. Breathing and swallowing become difficult, foaming at the mouth begins, and a fear of drinking liquids sets in. Two to ten days after the first symptoms appear, the patient becomes comatose and then dies. All rabies cases were fatal before Pasteur and Roux used their vaccine on humans in 1885.

For many diseases, people must receive the appropriate vaccine before becoming infected. However, it takes up to eight weeks for rabies to develop in a person, so the vaccine can be given after a person has been bitten by a rabid animal. Today, the vaccination of dogs and cats has reduced the number of deaths from rabies in North America to one or two a year. Most are caused by bat bites, which often go undetected and untreated.

enough after the bite, they became immune to the rabies virus already in their system. Three months earlier, Pasteur had saved nine-year-old Joseph Meister with this technique.

Attacked on July 4, 1885, Joseph had aggravated a dog by poking it with a stick, and the rabid dog had mauled him severely. On July 6, the young boy and his mother arrived at 45 Rue d'Ulm, Paris, France, Pasteur's laboratory, for help. Without the vaccine, the boy would surely die, but would the vaccine save him? Reluctantly, Pasteur agreed to treat the boy.

That night, Pasteur injected Joseph in the abdomen with the first of 14 injections of a weakened form of the rabies virus. This was the first time a person had received the rabies vaccine. Pasteur took a great risk in treating the boy. He was not a licensed physician and could have been arrested for administering medical treatment. But Pasteur had taken chances all his life. During his search for a treatment for rabies, he once sucked saliva from the mouth of a rabid dog. Axel Munthe, a Swedish physician who knew Pasteur, recalled:

> *Pasteur himself was absolutely fearless. Anxious to secure a sample of saliva straight from the jaws of a rabid dog, I once*

*saw him with the glass tube held between his lips draw a few
drops of the deadly saliva from the mouth of a rabid bulldog, held on the table by two assistants, their hands protected
by leather gloves.[2]*

Rather than let the Meister boy die, Pasteur ignored the possible consequences. In his laboratory notebook, he recorded a detailed account of Joseph's treatment. At the top of the first page, he wrote, "Production of the refractory state [unstable condition] in a child very dangerously bitten by a rabid dog."[3]

The treatment proved to be a great success, and Joseph escaped certain death. Pasteur was not prosecuted for what he did; he was praised as a hero.

Second Human Vaccinated

Three months after the Meister incident, Mayor Perrot pleaded with Pasteur to save the life of young Jean-Baptiste Jupille. Pasteur responded to Perrot immediately by letter. He told him the story of young Joseph and offered to treat the teenager. Jean-Baptiste boarded the next train to Paris.

Pasteur began treating the boy at his laboratory on October 20, 1885. Every day, Jean-Baptiste received an injection of the rabies vaccine. On the sixth day of treatment, Pasteur presented his findings in person to the French Academy of Sciences. He read from what became his famous paper that announced the administration of his rabies vaccine to humans. He declared:

> *After, I may say, innumerable experiments, I have at last found a method . . . that has already proved successful in the dog so constantly in so many cases that I feel confident of its general applicability to all animals and to man himself.*[4]

The audience stood and applauded. Three members spoke, expressing great admiration for Pasteur and his accomplishment. The second speaker was so moved by the report that he asked the academy to award Pasteur the national prize for virtue. Henri Bouley, president of the Academy of Science, called Pasteur's achievement "one of the greatest advances ever accomplished in the domain of medicine."[5]

News of Pasteur's amazing accomplishment spread quickly.

French Academy of Sciences

The French Academy of Sciences (*Académie des Sciences*) was founded in Paris in 1666 by France's King Louis XIV. The purpose of the academy was to encourage and protect the spirit of French scientific research.

Today, the academy has 150 full members, who are elected for life. It also has 300 corresponding members and 120 foreign associates. It is housed in the French Institute in Paris.

Victims of rabid animal bites from all over the world flocked to Paris for treatment. Rabies treatment centers were established in other countries. Within one year, the rabies vaccine had been administered to almost 2,500 people in Paris alone.

Monetary contributions poured in for Pasteur's work. With some of the money, Pasteur built the Pasteur Institute in Paris in 1887. In front of the building, he placed a statue of the shepherd boy Jean-Baptiste Jupille being attacked by a rabid dog. The institute would become an important center for research in the battle against diseases. It would also be a lasting tribute to Louis Pasteur, one of the great giants of science whose remarkable contributions helped save millions of lives all over the world.

Importance of the Experiment

Pasteur had a creative imagination and a logical mind. He used both to conduct precise experiments. He once said, "Imagination should give wings to our thoughts but we always need decisive experimental proof, and when the moment comes to draw conclusions and to interpret the gathered observations, imagination must be checked and dominated by the factual results of the experiment."[6]

A statue of Jean-Baptiste Jupille outside the Pasteur Institute tells the story of one of Pasteur's earliest rabies patients.

Arbois, France

A Tanner's Son

Jeanne-Etiennette Roqui, Louis Pasteur's mother, was a serious woman only interested in her household and her family. Louis's father, Jean-Joseph Pasteur, was a tanner as his father and grandfather had been.

Born on December 27, 1822, in Dole, France, Louis was the second child in the family. He had one sister, four-year-old Jeanne-Antoine, whom they called Virginie. When Louis was two, his sister Josephine was born. That year, his family moved to a modest house in nearby Marnoz, where his father set up a small tannery. The following year, his parents had another child, a girl named Emilie. In 1827, the family moved again, a few miles away to the town of Arbois.

Tanning Process

Tanners converted animal hides into leather by soaking them in a solution and then stretching them over a wooden log. The hides were then scraped with a dull sickle—a cutting instrument with a curved blade and a short handle. Once the skins were smooth, the tanner laid them out to dry.

LIFE IN ARBOIS

Jean-Joseph Pasteur rented a building in Arbois for his tannery. A quiet man, he was a hard worker and dedicated to producing the finest leather from animal hides. One day, Louis would tell his father:

And you, my dear father, . . . you showed me what patience can accomplish when the task is long. It is to you that I owe my tenacity [determination] in carrying out the work that needs to be done from day to day.[1]

The family's simple home was on the banks of the Cuisance River. The charming town was filled with vast vineyards that produced some of the finest French wines. The fields were in stark contrast to the steep cliffs that rose above the craggy banks of the river.

Louis grew up sledding in the snow, fishing from the bridge, and celebrating the fall wine grape harvests in town. On autumn days, carts bursting with ripe grapes clattered along the streets. In the evenings, townspeople enjoyed lavish banquets of French soups, wines, and cheeses.

School Days

At the age of eight, Louis started school, which was located in a spare room at the Arbois town hall. He was an average student, but he worked hard. His father tutored him at home to help him keep up with his studies. Louis was often interested in other activities, such as fishing, drawing, and painting. Some think he would have become a great artist if he had not been encouraged to study science. The headmaster of Louis's school recognized the boy's great potential. "One must not steer your son toward the chair of a small college like ours; he ought to be

Louis painted this portrait of his father, Jean-Joseph Pasteur.

[a] professor in a royal university," the headmaster told Jean-Joseph.[2] And to Louis he said, "My young friend, try for the great École Normale."[3] This elite institute of higher education in Paris was dedicated to teaching and research.

In October 1838, the 15-year-old Louis and his good friend Jules Vercel left Arbois to attend the Saint-Louis school in Paris. This school prepared students for institutions of higher education, such as the École Normale. Louis immediately became homesick and told Jules, "If I could only smell the odor of the tannery, . . . I am sure I would feel much better."[4] So great was his yearning for home that in mid-November, his father arrived in Paris to take his son back home to Arbois.

Pasteur the Artist

Louis Pasteur showed great promise as an artist. Some of his portraits were extremely sophisticated. On December 22, 1972, the 150th anniversary of Pasteur's birth, the cover of the *Science* journal featured a color reproduction of one of Pasteur's paintings—a portrait of Father Gaidot, a neighbor of the Pasteur family.

It would take time for Louis to recover from what he considered a failure. He spent most of his time drawing and painting; it was a healing therapy for him. He attended school in Arbois for one year but then had to decide whether he would go on to higher education. He chose the Royal College of Besançon, approximately 30 miles (48 km) from Arbois.

Although Louis was a good student at Besançon, he was better known as "the artist," the one who painted outstanding portraits of his classmates. "All this will not get

Louis loved being a student at the École Normale Supérieure.

me into the École Normale," he said. "I'd rather have the first place in college than ten thousand superficial compliments in society."[5] At the end of his first year, Louis received numerous awards in drawing, theology, Latin, physics, and mathematics. But before he could qualify for the École Normale, he needed a bachelor of science degree.

In 1842, at the age of 20, Pasteur received a degree in science. In 1843, he was accepted into the science department at the École Normale Supérieure in Paris. There, he began studying chemistry.

École Normale Supérieure

Today, the École Normale Supérieure in Paris continues to rank high among universities in the world. It provides a training-by-research education that encourages innovation and creativity. The college is considered the pinnacle of higher education in France. Acceptance is highly competitive and based on a student's intellectual potential.

ÉCOLE NORMALE SUPÉRIEURE

Pasteur was highly motivated to learn everything he could. Day and night he studied; he also tutored students at a boarding school. His father was worried about him, "You work immoderately," he wrote. "We are worried about your health. It isn't good to be always high-strung. Ruining your health is not the way to success!"[6]

Pasteur was becoming enthused about research and discovery. One biographer later wrote, "The passion—the almost insane urge—to move on into the unchartered lands of nature had taken hold of him."[7]

The Influence of Dumas

At the nearby Sorbonne, the University of Paris, Professor Jean-Baptiste-André Dumas attracted crowds of 600 to 700 students for his lectures. He was France's most celebrated chemist. Although Pasteur was a student at the École Normale, he regularly attended lectures at the Sorbonne given by Dumas out of a genuine love for science. Pasteur wanted to learn everything he could from Dumas, "who could set fire to the soul."[8] Addressing large audiences, Dumas conducted experiments with perfect accuracy. Pasteur took it all in.

Before Pasteur met Dumas, he wrote him a letter, asking to become his teaching assistant. He wrote that he wanted to devote his life to science and become a distinguished professor. Pasteur said he could perfect his teaching if he worked closely with Dumas.

Dumas and Pasteur shared an interest in molecules and other particles that could be seen only with a microscope. They also shared a desire to improve France's educational standards in science. Dumas once petitioned France to equip the Sorbonne with laboratories. Years later, Pasteur would do the same for the École Normale.

At the École Normale, another famous chemistry professor, Antoine-Jérôme Balard, took on Pasteur as his assistant in 1846. Pasteur spent all his spare time in Balard's laboratory where he conducted many chemical experiments on crystals.

DEATH OF HIS MOTHER

On May 21, 1848, Pasteur's mother became very ill. Pasteur left Paris and traveled to Arbois. He arrived too late; his mother had died from a massive stroke just before he arrived. Her untimely death may have been brought on by her worrying about her son in

Antoine-Jérôme Balard

When Pasteur was still a small boy, the then 24-year-old Antoine-Jérôme Balard (1802–1876), had become a well-known scientist. After gathering seawater and plants from the salt marshes near his home, Balard took them back to his laboratory. He wanted to determine whether there was something in seaweed other than iodine. He extracted a red fluid and discovered a new element. It would be called bromine. For the next 30 years, photographers such as Louis Daguerre used Balard's preparation of bromine to develop film.

Balard's discovery secured him the position of chair of chemistry for the faculty of sciences in Paris. Later, he was appointed professor of chemistry at the College of France. The French chemist significantly influenced Pasteur and encouraged his research.

Not only was Balard's lab simple, he encouraged his students to devise and build their own equipment. This suited Pasteur's inquiring, inventive mind. But he was not yet ready to take on a project of his own. Rather, he contributed to the work of his teachers. In 1848, in Balard's laboratory, Pasteur made his famous discoveries on the properties of crystals.

Paris. The peasants and working class were rioting in the streets, demonstrating against a new government that had imposed high taxes during tough economic times. Paris was not a safe place to be.

CRYSTALS

Six days before his mother's death, Pasteur had presented his astounding findings on crystals to the renowned Academy of Sciences. He reported that he had isolated two compounds found in wine: tartaric acid and paratartaric acid. Chemical analysis showed that the two compounds were identical. But Pasteur noticed that crystals formed by tartaric acid refracted light, while crystals from paratartaric acid did not.

Pasteur then carefully observed paratartaric acid under a microscope and found that it contained two types of crystals that were mirror images of each other. He separated the two crystals and observed how they reacted to light. By shining light through each crystal, Pasteur noticed that one crystal deflected light to the right; the other deflected light to the left. When they were combined, they canceled each other out, and no light was deflected.

His research encouraged scientists to consider the structure of molecules. This field of study came to be called stereochemistry. It advanced the study of the arrangement of atoms within molecules.

Return to Paris

Pasteur returned to Paris but constantly worried about his father. The rebellion was still going on, but Pasteur managed to focus on his research. He completed his doctoral thesis on crystals and received a doctor of science degree.

In January 1849, Pasteur began his position as assistant professor of chemistry at the University of Strasbourg in the Alsace region of France. He would continue his research on crystals. He would also meet his future wife. ⌐

A microscopic view of tartaric acid in wine

Pasteur's chemist bottles

Marriage and Children

asteur arrived at the University of Strasbourg on January 22, 1849. The university's rector, Mr. Laurent, welcomed Pasteur and invited him to his house. Pasteur was immediately attracted to Laurent's daughter, Marie.

Letter of Proposal

Within a few weeks, Pasteur wrote a letter to Mr. Laurent, asking for his daughter's hand in marriage. Pasteur told him about his father, the tanner; his sisters who still lived at home; and his mother who had died in May. He explained that his family was comfortable but not wealthy. He added that he had no possessions at all. He listed his only assets as "good health, an honest heart, and my position at the university."[1]

University of Strasbourg

Pasteur's influence as a professor at Strasbourg was significant. In the 1970s, the university was divided into three separate universities. One was called the Louis Pasteur University Institute of Technology, which focuses on research and teaching in natural sciences, technology, and medicine. Today, nearly 20,000 students attend the university.

Pasteur's letter also gave details about his education. He told Laurent that he planned to devote himself to chemical research and return to Paris one day. He made it clear that he loved science "for science's sake."[2] Weeks went by, and Pasteur received no answer to his letter. At the end of March, the 26-year-old Pasteur wrote to Marie's mother, "I am well aware that I lack the attributes that instantly attract a young girl. But experience tells me that when people get to know me well enough, they like me."[3] He also enclosed a letter to Marie. It was proper, at that time, for Mrs. Laurent to deliver the letter to her daughter. A courtship followed, and Pasteur expressed his love for Marie in a letter:

> *My dear Marie, . . . Thanks, a thousand thanks for your love.
> . . . I have only one thought: you. My work no longer means
> anything to me: I who so much loved my crystals, I who used
> to wish in the evening for a shorter night so that I could sooner
> be back at my studies.*[4]

LOUIS AND MARIE

Pasteur eventually received Mr. Laurent's approval to marry his daughter. On May 29, 1849, Louis Pasteur and Marie Laurent were married in Strasbourg at the Church of Sainte Madeleine. Pasteur was nearly late for his own wedding. He had been working in his laboratory all night, and a friend had to remind him to go to the church that morning for his wedding ceremony.

In April 1850, Louis and Marie became parents of a baby girl they named Jeanne. Marie took care of the household and the new baby. She understood her husband's passion for science and realized he needed to be learning, researching, and working constantly. She spent time with him by helping him with his work in the evenings. Louis dictated notes and letters, and Marie wrote them down. She was genuinely interested in her husband's research. They were right for each other. The marriage would last 46 years—the rest of Pasteur's life.

CHILDREN AND PROMOTIONS

In October 1851, Louis and Marie had their second child, a boy named Jean-Baptiste. The following year, in November 1852, Pasteur was promoted to full professor of chemistry at the University of Strasbourg. In October 1853, the Pasteurs had another child, a daughter named Cécile. In 1854, Pasteur became a professor of chemistry and the dean of science at the University of Lille in Lille, France.

Pasteur's lectures drew large crowds of students

A Man of Repute

By his early thirties, Pasteur had already gained an incredible reputation. The rector of the University of Lille wrote:

Pasteur is a very distinguished scientist and an outstanding teacher. . . . His lectures are admirably prepared, his experiments made with extraordinary skill and complete success. . . . I might add that . . . Pasteur has a passion for the science he is teaching; . . . that he is doing research work which, day by day, contributes to the value of his lectures.[5]

Pasteur did not confine himself to his laboratory and theories. He was also interested in delving into more practical issues and problems that affected local farmers and businesses.

who were fascinated with his courses in chemistry, physics, and natural history. It was one of his students who caused Pasteur to shift his interest from crystals to fermentation.

The student's father, Monsieur Bigo, added yeast to beet juice, which changed the sugar in the juice into alcohol. He then sold the alcohol for a living. However, some of the juice mysteriously turned sour during the fermenting process. Intrigued by these facts, Pasteur now focused his research on fermentation issues. Little did he know that his experiments with alcohol would not only explain fermentation but would lead to the discovery of bacteria. One day, it would help him solve some of the mysteries of contagious diseases.

"When I approach a child, he inspires in me two sentiments; tenderness for what he is, and respect for what he may become."[6]

—Louis Pasteur

12 Février 1861. MM. Dumas, Balard et

Notes written by Pasteur

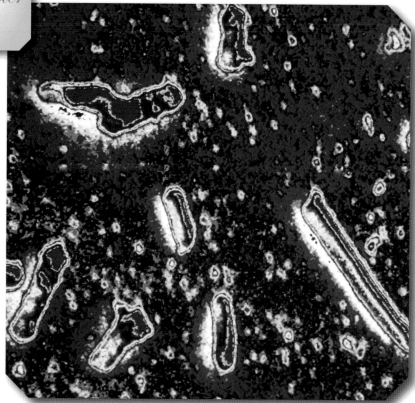

A view of rod-shaped bacteria through a modern electron microscope

FERMENTATION AND
BACTERIA

In the fall of 1856, Pasteur visited the
brewery where Bigo turned beet juice
into alcohol. With only a little stove and a small
microscope, Pasteur went to work. He repeatedly
observed fermenting juice under his microscope

and finally declared that what he saw were living organisms—one-celled fungi called yeast. These were growing and multiplying. Pasteur concluded that these tiny, active, living cells caused the sugar in the beet juice to convert to alcohol.

For thousands of years, people had used yeast to make bread dough rise, ferment drinks, and make cheese out of milk. Grape growers had also used yeast to turn grape juice into wine for centuries, but no one knew why the fermentation process worked. In 1680, nearly 200 years before Pasteur's discovery, Dutch scientist Antoni van Leeuwenhoek had observed yeast under a microscope, but he had not considered it a living organism. No one knew that living microorganisms constantly changed the makeup of juices and foods.

Although Pasteur knew the living yeast cells caused fermentation, he visited the brewery for a different reason. He wanted to determine why some of the alcohol was turning sour. Looking at the spoiled alcohol under a microscope, Pasteur observed yeast cells, but he also saw smaller, rod-shaped cells. These one-celled organisms were bacteria.

Bacteria

In late 1857, Pasteur returned to Paris. He had been appointed assistant director of scientific studies at his alma mater, the École Normale Supérieure. There, Pasteur continued his experiments on fermentation and bacteria. Since the school did not provide a laboratory for him, he found two small, abandoned rooms in the school's attic and converted them into a lab. He paid for most of the equipment with his own money.

Eventually, Pasteur was furnished with space for a larger laboratory. It consisted of five narrow rooms on two floors, and Pasteur spent countless hours experimenting and observing microorganisms. Still lacking adequate space, Pasteur conducted some of his experiments under the stairway. He had to crawl on his hands and knees to check the incubator where bacteria were growing. In these challenging circumstances, Pasteur made discoveries that would be the foundation for the rest of his work.

JOY AND SORROW

The Pasteur family was growing. In July 1858, their fourth child, Marie Louise, was born. Louis and Marie enjoyed their four children and found great joy in family life. However, their joy was replaced with sorrow. In August 1859, when Pasteur was in Paris for examinations, their oldest child, Jeanne, contracted typhoid fever. She died in September and was buried in Arbois. Extremely distraught, Pasteur wrote,

> I heard the sound of the coffin and of the cords that took it down to the bottom of her grave, and the sound of the earth falling on that wood, both so empty and so full. [2]

To his wife, Marie, he wrote of hope:

> I wish that between us, with us, there will be nothing but our love, our children, their upbringing, their future, along with my dreams of science. For you, for them, life will be made beautiful by my work, by the success of new discoveries, and by generous feelings. [3]

In the years to come, Pasteur's loss would increase his passion for discovery. The death of his daughter Jeanne created a deep desire to study diseases. One day, he would passionately search for ways to protect people, especially children, from deadly

Pasteur working in his lab

illnesses. For now, Pasteur found some comfort in his personal faith in God and turned to his work for relief from his sorrow.

SPONTANEOUS GENERATION

There was a controversy among the scientific community. For centuries, some people had believed in the theory of spontaneous generation—the common belief that sometimes plants and animals developed from nonliving things.

Some scientists believed that frogs developed out of sticky mud at the bottom of marshes. Others claimed that mice could develop in 21 days in a sealed pot full of corn and a dirty shirt. Now, in the mid-nineteenth century, the French Academy of Sciences wanted to prove whether the theory of spontaneous generation was right or wrong. The academy sponsored a contest and offered prize money to the scientist who could produce proof either way.

Pasteur believed the issue must be resolved once and for all. He put his studies on fermentation and bacteria aside to begin his investigation of spontaneous generation. He relied on scientific experimentation to find his answers.

Aristotle

As early as the fourth century BCE, Greek philosopher Aristotle stated that some animals "spring from parent animals" and others "grow spontaneously . . . from putrefying [rotting] earth or vegetable matter, as is the case with a number of insects."[4] Aristotle also believed that new life could form from the secretions inside animal organs.

THE SWAN-NECKED FLASK

In 1859, Pasteur made a swan-necked flask. It was a special glass bulb with a long, tapered, hollow neck that rose up and then curved down and around twice in the shape of the letter S. The end was open to allow air in from the outside. Pasteur filled the flask with beef broth. He knew that meat broth exposed to air would grow organisms such as mold. Science at the time believed such organisms to be the product of spontaneous generation.

Pasteur set out to prove otherwise—that mold grew from bacteria in the air. He heated the broth solution to its boiling point, simmering it for several minutes. The heat killed any bacteria present in the broth.

For several months, the liquid did not change. Pasteur discovered that the S-shaped glass neck allowed air into the flask but trapped airborne germs at the bottom of each curve. Bacteria could not get into the broth. When Pasteur tipped the flask and allowed the liquid to touch the trapped germs, the broth became contaminated with bacteria and began to spoil. Pasteur concluded that as long as the liquid was protected from bacteria in the air, it remained sterile, or pure.

Pasteur tested his experiment in a variety of surroundings—in the city, in the country, and at the top of high mountains. He tested it indoors and outdoors. He learned that bacteria grew more readily in flasks in cities than on mountain tops. Other scientists worked to prove that spontaneous generation of living things was possible. French journalists followed the competition and the debate, filling French newspapers with coverage.

In April 1864, Pasteur presented the results of his experiment to a large audience at the Sorbonne in Paris. He displayed flasks of beef broth that were four years old and still clear, sterile, unspoiled, and unfermented. He explained that he had "kept it away from the germs in the air, kept it away from life."[5] Pasteur's experiments showed that when living organisms such as bacteria and fungi are kept out of food, the food does not grow any organisms such as mold. It does not change at all.

Billions of Bacteria

Billions of bacteria are found in soil, water, and all living things. Many bacteria are essential for good health in humans. The immune system protects the body from most harmful bacteria. However, a few bacteria are pathogens that cause infectious diseases, such as typhoid fever, cholera, tetanus, diphtheria, syphilis, and tuberculosis.

Pasteur had proven the theory of spontaneous generation to be false. That summer, he presented his findings to the French Academy of Sciences. He produced flasks filled with liquid that had been purified by boiling. After three years, no new life had grown in the flasks. Pasteur convinced the academy of his theory. He received the Alhumbert Prize, a sum of money. The academy also awarded him the Jecker Prize for his findings on fermentation.

IMPROVING FRANCE'S WINE INDUSTRY

Pasteur was becoming a well-known scientist. France's Emperor Napoléon III greatly admired Pasteur. In 1864, the emperor asked Pasteur to investigate what was destroying the excellent quality of French wines. Some wines turned to acid with a bitter or sour taste; others became flat to the taste. Pasteur was glad to help France's wine industry.

Because of his experiments on the fermentation of beet juice, Pasteur immediately understood the cause of the wine problem. He said, "Each wine is being attacked by a specific kind of germ and is being fermented—or changed—into another substance."[6]

Pasteur set out to visit vineyards all over France and Belgium to determine which germs caused which problems. By early 1865, he made drawings of the germs that were to blame. "First, here are the fellows who swim about in the wines gone bitter," he said to fellow chemist Émile Duclaux. "Have you ever seen things that resembled infinitesimal [extremely small] strings of spaghetti more than they? And here are the ones in the acid-tasting wines."[7]

Pasteur declared that each problem was caused by a different bacterium. He conducted

Napoléon III

Louis-Napoléon, the nephew of Napoléon I, was born in 1808 and brought up in Switzerland. He attended various schools throughout Europe. In 1848, he was elected president of France. According to France's constitution, the length of the term was four years, and only one term was allowed. Not being able to run for election again, he gathered the support of the army, much of the lower class, and the working class. In December 1851, he seized control of the government. One year later, he became Emperor Napoléon III.

As emperor of France from 1852 to 1870, he sent French troops to participate in various wars, including those in the Crimea and Italy. His troops were not successful in Mexico—the French army experienced its first defeat in 50 years. In the 1860s, he ordered Paris to be cleaned up by getting rid of slums, widening streets, and building parks. Napoléon III also understood the importance of preserving historic buildings such as Notre Dame Cathedral. He ordered the construction of a modern sewage system to improve health and living conditions and was responsible for the French railroad system. Under his leadership, France's industries and economy improved.

numerous experiments in a crude laboratory in
Arbois, the town of his childhood and an area
famous for its wines. He wanted to find a way to
destroy the harmful bacteria in wine and keep
wine pure.

Unwelcome germs were always present on ripe
grapes that grew in the open air. Other bacteria
were introduced into wine vats from the hands of
workers or from the wine presses themselves. Pasteur
found that by heating wine for several minutes to
131 degrees Fahrenheit (55°C), the wine stayed pure.
The heat killed the bacteria and allowed the wine to
be stored indefinitely. The heating process did not
alter the wine's flavor in any way. Pasteur called in
wine experts to taste heated wine and compare it to
unheated wine. The experts agreed that heat did not
change the taste or quality of the wine.

Makers of wine, as well as beer, began heating
all their alcohol in large vats. Pasteur's book, *Studies
in Wine*, clearly described the process. Winemakers
could follow the instructions and learn how to heat
wine before bottling it. The process came to be
called pasteurization—named after Louis Pasteur.

*Pasteur used this swan-necked flask in his experiments
with bacteria and sterilization.*

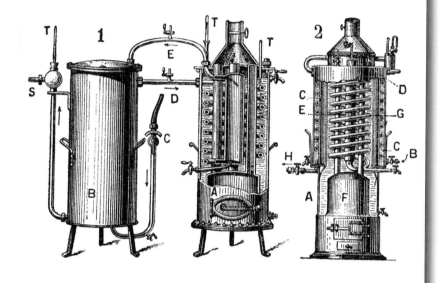

Pasteur's invention for sterilization

Saving France's
Industries

The pasteurization process improved
France's wine and beer industries. It also
worked in the dairy industry with milk and cream.
Dairy farmers found that heating milk to a specific
temperature killed most of the bad bacteria and

lengthened the time it took for milk to spoil.

DISEASED SILKWORMS

The people of France were grateful to Pasteur for saving some of their country's largest industries. But now another industry needed his help—the silk industry. In 1865, France's minister of agriculture asked Pasteur to determine why the nation's silkworms were dying.

Since at least the fifteenth century, France had been a leading producer of silk. Thousands of people were employed in the silk textile industry. Now silkworms were dying of a disease called pébrine, and no one knew what to do. Over a period of 20 years, the disease had spread to silkworms all over the world, including those in Italy, Spain, Austria, Turkey, and China. In some instances, pébrine caused brown and black spots to appear on

Pasteurized Milk

The most common effect of bacteria in milk is souring. Bacteria convert sugar in milk into lactic acid, which curdles milk and gives it a sour taste. Pasteurization of milk, called High Temperature Short Time (HTST), kills 99.99 percent of harmful microorganisms. It destroys nearly all yeasts, mold, and bacteria that cause milk to spoil or cause diseases. Some microorganisms have become resistant to heat. Scientists are looking for ways to destroy these disease-causing bacteria that survive pasteurization.

the worms, but not all diseased silkworms had these spots. Pébrine also made it impossible for silkworms to spin silk fiber, the strands of silk that are used to weave silk fabric.

The Making of Silk

Spinning silk is essential to the life cycle of a silkworm (*Bombyx mori*). Although many insects produce silk, the silk from *Bombyx mori* is the only silk used by the commercial silk industry. Silkworms are the larvae of silk moths. They grow on a diet of mulberry leaves. Eventually, silkworms encase themselves in cocoons that they spin by moving their heads in a figure-eight pattern. Their glands produce liquid silk strands that form the cocoon. Within three days, a silkworm can spin approximately one mile (1.61 km) of continuous silk fiber.

Inside the cocoon, the silkworm grows to be a moth. Normally, the moth makes a hole in the cocoon so it can get out. This cuts the silk threads and ruins them. Silk producers do not allow the moth to break out of its cocoon. Instead, they drop the cocoon into boiling water before the moth makes a hole in it. The moth inside dies, but the silk of the cocoon is saved. The silk producer then carefully unwinds the long strand of silk fiber from the cocoon. Since the thread is so thin, several strands of silk are spun together to form one silk thread. The silk thread is then woven into fine silk fabric.

LABORATORY IN ALÈS

Pasteur immediately set out to attempt to save the country's silk industry. If he found a solution to the pébrine issue, several other countries that depended on silk production would also benefit. In June 1865, Pasteur and three of his assistants traveled to Alès, the center of France's silkworm industry.

The silkworm cultivators were discouraged and skeptical. They did not believe that a chemist who knew nothing about silkworms could help them.

Pasteur convinced the cultivators that he was their only hope to save the silkworm. They agreed to cooperate and gave him a chance. With several microscopes, Pasteur's team set up a makeshift laboratory. The cultivators brought in both healthy and diseased silkworms for study under a microscope. Pasteur immediately discovered that certain corpuscles, or globs of cells, were present in the diseased worms but not in the healthy ones. When a worm died of pébrine, it was filled with these corpuscles.

Pasteur's next step was to experiment with the corpuscles to determine whether they were contagious. He found that when a diseased worm scratched a healthy worm, the healthy worm was quickly infected. Thus, Pasteur determined that pébrine was highly contagious. He suggested that all diseased eggs and the parent silkworms be destroyed. The spread of the disease would be reduced significantly.

Pasteur returned to Paris the summer of 1865 with a set of healthy silkworms. He intended to

Items used by Pasteur in his laboratory

continue studying the worms and to return to Alès
the following year to check on the spread of pébrine.

DISEASE HITS HOME

Two years before the Pasteurs had returned to
Paris, they had another child. A baby girl, Camille,
was born on July 8, 1863. But in 1865, two-year-old
Camille became very ill. It had been six years since
the Pasteurs' daughter Jeanne had died of typhoid
fever. Now Pasteur feared he would lose a second
child. On September 11, 1865, little Camille died

of a tumor on the liver. Filled with grief, rage, and hopelessness, Pasteur was "stunned by pain."[1] He wrote to his favorite professor, Jean-Baptiste-André Dumas:

> *My poor child died this morning; she was so lucid [alert] to the very end that when her little hands were getting cold, she constantly asked to place them into mine, which she had never done throughout her long illness.*[2]

Typhoid Fever

Typhoid fever is a deadly disease caused by the bacterium *Salmonella typhi*. The disease is spread by contaminated food or water. Drinking water contaminated by sewage containing the bacteria can spread the disease rapidly. Infected people experience a high fever, stomach pains, headache, and sometimes a rash.

The Pasteurs buried Camille in Arbois. Three months earlier, Pasteur had mourned at the same cemetery for his father, who had died on June 15.

Eight months after the death of Camille, the Pasteurs lost a third daughter. Cécile died May 23, 1866, of typhoid fever. She was 12. Her body was buried in Arbois next to her two sisters and her grandfather. In great despair, Pasteur wrote to his wife:

> *My dearest Marie, so they will all die one by one, our dear children, you my poor Cécile whom I loved so much, and you two others who are already gone and who call her to be with you. I too long to join you, my dear children.*[3]

In less than seven years, the Pasteurs had lost three of their five children. Only two remained—Jean-Baptiste and Marie Louise. How could a famous scientist such as Pasteur find cures for sour wine and diseased silkworms and not be able to save his own children? His passion grew to find a cure for diseases.

In 1865, a cholera epidemic swept through Europe and Paris, and hundreds of people perished. Pasteur began working even harder in his laboratory. Work helped him blot out his sorrows, but it also prepared him to one day wage war against the diseases that were ravaging his family and his country.

Solution for Silkworms

In 1866 and 1867, Pasteur returned to Alès to check on the silkworm situation. Unfortunately, his plan to save silkworms was not working. Silkworm cultivators had

An Epidemic

Cholera is an infection of the intestine that causes diarrhea, vomiting, and abdominal pain. Due to these symptoms, a person loses body fluids, becomes dehydrated, and can die. The bacteria that causes the infection is often due to drinking water that is tainted by sewage or waste from a person who is already infected with the disease.

Today, proper water treatment and sanitation processes have greatly reduced the number of people who contract the disease.

Bombyx mori *cocoons*

done what Pasteur had suggested, but their silkworms were still dying. Eventually, Pasteur realized that France's silkworms had two diseases—pébrine and flacherie. The second disease was caused by bacteria that attacked the worms' intestines.

Pasteur gathered some silkworm eggs that were disease-free and took them to his laboratory. In a controlled environment, he allowed the eggs to hatch and continue through their entire life cycle. When he had enough eggs, he gave them to the silkworm

cultivators for the next season in
1868. He taught the cultivators how
to examine eggs under a microscope
for disease. If they saw organisms
that belonged to either disease, they
were to get rid of the eggs. They kept
only disease-free eggs. The number
of diseased silkworms eventually
decreased. France's silkworm industry
had been saved.

A New Laboratory
and a New Challenge

At the beginning of 1868, Pasteur
began a long struggle with the French
government to provide him with a
laboratory. After all, his work was
helping France with its industries
and economy. Finally, Emperor
Napoléon III ordered a laboratory
to be built for Pasteur in Paris in the
garden of the École Normale at 45
Rue d'Ulm. Pasteur was extremely
excited to finally have sufficient space
for his experiments. He worked

What Is a Stroke?

A stroke occurs when a
blood vessel is blocked
or bursts, reducing blood
flow to the brain. Part of
the brain cannot func-
tion, and usually one side
of the body is paralyzed.
Strokes are the leading
cause of adult disability
in the United States and
Europe.

tirelessly to design his lab and used his own money to furnish it.

On the morning of October 19, 1868, however, a very tired 46-year-old Pasteur experienced a strange tingling sensation on the left side of his body. He tried to ignore it all day. But that night, shortly after he went to bed, he had intermittent periods of paralysis. Several times, he lost control of his muscles on his left side; he also lost the ability to speak. His wife, Marie, asked their good friend Dr. Godélier to come to the house. Godélier told her that Louis was experiencing a cerebral hemorrhage—commonly known as a stroke. Marie did not believe her husband was going to survive.

The government did not expect Pasteur to live, either, and construction on his laboratory stopped. For seven days, Pasteur was close to death. But then he began to regain strength. Whenever he could

École Normale Laboratory

After his stroke, Pasteur was aware that the construction of his laboratory had stopped. The government and others expected that he would die. Pasteur, however, had a different opinion and complained of the work stoppage to his friend, General Fave. The general agreed to let the government know about the issue.

A few days later, Victor Duruy, minister of Public Instruction, received a note stating: "I have heard that ... the men who were working at M. Pasteur's laboratory were kept away from the very day he became ill; he has been much affected by this ... I beg you will issue orders that the work begun should be continued."[4] The note was signed by Emperor Napoléon III.

talk, he discussed his work. His students came to see him and wrote down everything he was able to say.

By January 1869, Pasteur was back at work studying silkworms. He had recovered from his stroke, although he walked with a limp and suffered from fatigue. His plan for producing healthy worms was working. That year, the French government approved his method. Pasteur had saved France's wine industry as well as its silk industry. Both industries had nearly failed, but now they were growing and prospering. In the eyes of the French people, Pasteur was a hero. ⌒

After his stroke, Pasteur dictated notes to his wife, regarding silkworms.

A painting of the siege of Paris during the Franco-Prussian War

THE FIGHT AGAINST GERMS

In 1870, Pasteur's new laboratory at the École Normale was completed. But instead of quietly enjoying his research, Pasteur watched as war broke out in France. On July 19, France declared war against Prussia—the Franco-Prussian War had

begun. Students of the École Normale went home
or enlisted in the French army. Pasteur's son, Jean-
Baptiste, enlisted and fought on the front lines. The
École Normale was turned into a hospital to treat
wounded French soldiers.

THE FRANCO-PRUSSIAN WAR

The French army was being pushed back, and the
enemy was advancing toward Paris. In September,
Pasteur and his wife left Paris for Arbois. Pasteur
was restless there, however, and could not work.
He worried that their son would be killed in battle.
The Pasteurs had not heard from Jean-Baptiste for
more than a month. In January 1871, they set out by
carriage to find their son and bring him home.

On the way, they saw exhausted and wounded
French soldiers retreating from battle. The tattered
soldiers begged for food, warm clothing, and
bandages for their frostbitten feet. Wherever they
went, Louis and Marie asked whether anyone had
seen Sergeant Pasteur. Finally, they found their thin,
weak son in the back of a wagon. They put him into
their carriage and returned to Arbois. At the end
of January, while Jean-Baptiste was still recovering,
France surrendered.

A War on Germs

Even though Arbois was now occupied by the Prussian army, Pasteur kept working as though nothing had changed. He began teaching brewers how to pasteurize their beer. In 1873, Pasteur was elected to the National Academy of Medicine, even though he was not a doctor. He hoped to work with doctors to study bacteria and diseases. He encouraged doctors to avoid germs and thus reduce infection and illness. Many doctors did not heed his advice.

To most people, hospitals were known as places where people died. Doctors and nurses did not wash their hands before or after surgery, and surgical instruments were not washed or sterilized. Bandages on patients were not changed very often, and hospitals were dirty. Most medical workers did not believe there was any connection between germs and infection or disease.

National Academy of Medicine

The National Academy of Medicine was founded in 1820 by King Louis XVIII. Its mission was to respond to requests from the French government concerning public health and epidemics or diseases in humans and animals. The academy also evaluated new medicines and made contributions to improve the art of healing.

Dr. Joseph Lister, an English physician, was working in Scotland. He was interested in what Pasteur had written about germs. Lister began requiring all surgical instruments in his hospital to be sterilized with carbolic acid. He required doctors and nurses to wash their hands before and after surgery. He insisted that patients' bandages be changed frequently and that the hospital be cleaner. Within two years, surgical deaths at Lister's hospital dropped from 45 percent to 15 percent. In 1874, Dr. Lister wrote a letter to Pasteur:

Is It Sterilized?

Today there are a variety of ways to sterilize surgical instruments and medications. Harmful bacteria, viruses, fungi, and spores can be destroyed by heat, chemicals, radiation, or filtering. For best results, sterilization is conducted in a room in which the air has been filtered to remove almost all airborne particles.

Allow me to take this opportunity to tender you my most cordial thanks for having, by your brilliant researches, demonstrated to me the truth of the germ theory. . . . It would, I believe, give you sincere gratification to see at our hospital how largely mankind is being benefited by your labours. I need hardly add that it would afford me the highest gratification to show you how greatly surgery is indebted to you. [1]

Word of Lister's antiseptic methods spread quickly. Some younger doctors began using his techniques and credited Pasteur for teaching them about germs.

PERSISTENT PASTEUR

Most doctors in the Academy of Medicine, however, did not believe that a mere chemist, as they called Pasteur, could teach them anything about medicine. But Pasteur persisted in telling them about the dangers of germs. At a meeting of the academy, Pasteur interrupted a doctor who was lecturing on the causes of childbirth fever. New mothers were dying of the fever by the hundreds in Paris alone. Pasteur boldly walked onto the platform and announced that the speaker was wrong. Then he began drawing on a chalkboard what he had seen with his microscope in every case of the fever. They were germs—small, round

Listerine

Dr. Joseph Lister has been called the father of modern antisepsis, which is the destruction of disease-causing microorganisms. He noticed that fewer babies died when they were delivered by midwives. Midwives washed their hands more often than surgeons did. In 1879, Listerine mouthwash was named after him for his pioneering use of antiseptics.

Pasteur in his laboratory at the École Normale

microorganisms clinging to each other in long
strands.

Most of the doctors shouted insults at Pasteur
and told him to take his germs back to his laboratory.
They believed germs were too small to have any effect
on their patients. Angered, Pasteur left the meeting.
But he did not give up trying to convince doctors
to wash their hands and sterilize their equipment.
He now put all his time and energy into germs and
diseases that were afflicting humans and animals. He
would start with animals.

FINDING ANSWERS

By 1877, Pasteur's laboratory had taken on a new look. Against one wall was a row of pens filled with bleating sheep. Some of the sheep were sick, wracked with pain from anthrax, a disease that was killing thousands of France's sheep. Across the lab, cages housed rabid dogs. Froth spilled from their mouths while they thrashed their bodies against the steel bars of their cages. Their eyes rolled around dizzily while they growled and snarled. If bitten by a dog with rabies, a person would die

Deadly Anthrax

Most forms of anthrax are deadly and affect humans as well as animals. Spores of anthrax bacteria can survive harsh conditions for long periods of time. The spores can be inhaled. Most anthrax infects animals that eat or inhale the spores while grazing outdoors. Anthrax is also spread when one animal eats an infected animal. Today, anthrax is quite rare in humans.

Anthrax spores can be developed in a laboratory and used as a biological weapon. Just one week after the September 11, 2001, terrorist attacks, letters containing anthrax spores were sent to NBC's news anchor, Tom Brokaw, and the *New York Post*. Over the next few weeks, other letters containing anthrax were sent through the mail. Two were addressed to politicians—Senators Tom Daschle and Patrick Leahy. Several letters were addressed to news agencies. Five people who had handled the letters died from the anthrax, two of whom were postal workers. Seventeen others were infected but survived. A 2004 study increased that number to 68. In 2008, Bruce Edwards Ivins was arrested as a suspect in the anthrax attacks. He was a scientist at the US biodefense labs at Fort Detrick in Frederick, Maryland. Before Ivins could be tried, he committed suicide.

an agonizing death from fever and hydrophobia, an extreme fear of drinking water.

Pasteur set aside his work on fermentation to focus completely on diseases. The passion that had been born in him after the deaths of his three daughters had taken root and was growing. He would study anthrax first.

DYING SHEEP

Sheep were dying at a high rate throughout France. Some farmers were losing 20 out of every 100 sheep to the deadly anthrax disease. Cattle, horses, and sometimes humans were also contracting this highly contagious disease characterized by fever, swelling throat, shaking limbs, and, finally, death within a few hours.

Pasteur began his experiments. Using a microscope, he observed sheep blood that was swarming with rod-shaped microorganisms called rods. He also saw small oval-shaped organisms called spores. As the organisms grew, they looked like long worms tangled together in a maze. Next, Pasteur took a tiny drop of the blood and weakened it in another solution. He weakened the blood 40 times, transferring a drop into another solution each time.

All that remained in the solution were a few rods and spores.

Pasteur injected the weakened solution into some healthy rabbits and guinea pigs. All of the animals sickened and died. Now he knew that the rods and spores were the cause of anthrax. But he still did not know how to prevent animals from getting the disease. He would discover that in another experiment. ⌐

Dr. Joseph Lister

Dr. Émile Roux was one of Pasteur's assistants.

TACKLING CONTAGIOUS DISEASES

In 1879, Pasteur visited a chicken farm on the outskirts of Paris. Six dead hens were inside the chicken coop. More chickens were in a fenced area behind the farmhouse. They were alive but very sick. Some lay motionlessness; others staggered about with heads hung low and feathers ruffled. Pasteur knew what they had—chicken cholera.

Pasteur immediately returned to his lab with some healthy chickens and some sick ones. He put his assistants—Émile Roux and Charles Chamberland—to work making room for chicken cages. Then he told them to look through a microscope for long periods of time at germs taken from the diseased chickens. He wanted them to watch how the germs changed and grew. For weeks, the scientists observed the microorganisms. But the solution to the cholera dilemma came about purely by accident.

French Poultry Industry

In 1871, France produced an enormous amount of eggs and poultry. France exported more than $6 million worth of eggs to England. Today, poultry remains an important industry in France. The average person eats 51 pounds (23 kg) of poultry a year. However, in 2005, when fears arose about the avian (bird) flu, France's $10 billion poultry industry was hit hard.

SOLUTION TO CHOLERA

One day, Pasteur told Roux to inject some healthy chickens with cholera germs that had been left standing in the open air for several weeks. Surprisingly, the chickens became sick but recovered the next day. Pasteur wondered whether the old germs were too weak to give them the disease or whether the old germs had made them immune to cholera.

Several weeks later, Pasteur went further with his experiment. He injected a strong dose of cholera into four healthy chickens. Two of these chickens had survived the injections of old cholera germs weeks earlier. The next day, Pasteur greeted his assistants, Roux and Chamberland, with the news. He pointed out that the new birds they had inoculated were dead. More

Pasteur's Colleagues

Pierre-Paul-Émile Roux was a physician, bacteriologist, immunologist, and Pasteur's closest colleague. In collaboration with other scientists, he demonstrated that a toxin produced by bacteria caused disease. The next step was to develop an antitoxin to treat diseases such as anthrax. Pasteur and Roux worked together from 1878 to 1883. Roux was a cofounder and integral part of the Pasteur Institute for 40 years.

Charles Chamberland, a microbiologist, was a specialist in bacteria, viruses, and fungi. In 1879, he invented an autoclave. This device sterilized equipment and instruments with high-pressured steam at high temperatures. In 1884, three years after working with Pasteur on the anthrax vaccine, Chamberland developed the Chamberland filter. The pores of the filter were so small that bacteria could not pass through it. When liquid was poured through the filter, harmful bacteria and other microorganisms were trapped in the filter.

Louis Thuillier, a biologist, began working for Pasteur in 1880. He traveled throughout France and Hungary vaccinating animals for anthrax and regularly wrote letters to Pasteur. The letters, which detailed the successes and failures of the vaccine, were published later as *Correspondence of Pasteur and Thuillier, Concerning Anthrax and Swine Fever Vaccinations.* In 1883, while studying cholera, Thuillier contracted the disease and died at the age of 27.

important, the chickens that had received an earlier smaller dose survived the lethal dose.

Roux and Chamberland were still puzzled. Pasteur explained that by making the animal sick with a weakened version of the virus, its body could fight it off. That meant that if the animal was exposed to the virus later, its body was immune to the disease.

Pasteur understood the implications and importance of this discovery. He had discovered a vaccine—a way to make chickens immune to cholera. A vaccine would save the lives of animals.

Cholera Vaccine

Pasteur, Roux, and Chamberland tested the vaccine right away. They injected old cholera bacteria into dozens of healthy chickens. All of these chickens became sick but quickly recovered. A few days later, the scientists injected a strong dose of fresh cholera bacteria into the vaccinated chickens. All tolerated the lethal dosage without becoming sick or dying. Pasteur was convinced he had found a cholera vaccine. He excitedly proclaimed to his colleagues:

*My friends, we are the most fortunate men in Europe. . . .
We've stumbled upon a protective vaccine—the cholera germs*

themselves! The weakened germs enable the animal to fight off their more powerful brothers. They are traitors to their own kind.[1]

Pasteur had turned harmful microorganisms against themselves. Now he wondered whether vaccines could be made to protect animals and humans from other diseases.

By early 1880, the chicken cholera vaccine had been perfected. Chickens all over France were being vaccinated against cholera. Pasteur enthusiastically presented his findings to the Academy of Medicine. The doctors still were not interested. Dr. Jules Guérin, a doctor in his eighties, stood up and said, "I am thoroughly bored by all this nonsensical fussing with mere chickens!"[2]

Not the First Vaccine

Pasteur's vaccines were not the first to be developed. In 1796, English physician Edward Jenner noticed that milkmaids who got a skin disease called cowpox did not get smallpox, the human equivalent. Jenner used the cowpox virus to vaccinate people against smallpox. The vaccine was used until 1974.

Guérin and Pasteur nearly entered into a fistfight over the matter, but their friends broke the two apart. Pasteur stomped out of the room, angry and humiliated. His most amazing discovery had been mocked. The joy of his achievement had been ruined. But he knew he was right, and he did not give up.

THE ANTHRAX CHALLENGE

Pasteur believed he could make other vaccines for other diseases. Anthrax was still running rampant throughout France. He believed a vaccine could protect sheep, cows, and horses from the deadly disease. He confidently announced his claim wherever he went. He had developed a weakened culture of anthrax that was strong enough to provide immunity. But there were still times that the injection of anthrax killed the animal. One skeptical horse doctor, Dr. Hippolyte Rossignol, challenged Pasteur to a public experiment. He wanted Pasteur to fail in front of a large crowd so he would stop talking about his vaccines.

Rossignol arranged for the Agricultural Society of Melun to buy animals for the public experiment. Pasteur accepted the challenge. He was confident that the vaccine, which had worked in his laboratory, would work at Melun. And, unlike the 14 sheep in the laboratory, he was willing to test it on 60 animals.

At Pouilly-le-Fort, a farm a few miles outside Melun, Pasteur planned a trial demonstration. Half of the animals would be vaccinated with a weakened dose of anthrax. The remaining animals would not be vaccinated. Later, Pasteur would inject all the animals with a strong, deadly dose of anthrax. A confident Pasteur predicted that the vaccinated animals would live and that the animals that were not vaccinated would all die within two days. Roux and Chamberland got the vaccines ready.

On May 5, 1881, the day to vaccinate the animals, the road to the farm was packed with hundreds of carriages and horses. Pasteur walked to the center of the farmyard and bowed. The large audience consisted of politicians, scientists, doctors, farmers, dignitaries, and journalists with notebooks and pencils. A few people cheered; many snickered. Then the animals were brought in. Pasteur and his colleagues began injecting half of the animals with the anthrax vaccine. A distinguishing mark was placed on each vaccinated animal.

Twelve days later, on May 17, 1881, the crowd convened again for the second round of injections. Huge doses of deadly anthrax were injected into all the animals. On June 2, a much larger crowd assembled to view the results of the experiment. Dr. Rossignol, who had set Pasteur up for failure, also attended. The crowd was astonished at what they saw. All of the animals that had received the

Pasteur vaccinates animals against anthrax.

vaccination of weakened anthrax were alive and healthy. But by the end of the day, all of the animals that had not been vaccinated were dead. They lay on the ground with gooey, black blood oozing from their noses and mouths.

The crowd roared for Pasteur and threw their hats in the air. The people of France went wild, shook Pasteur's hand, and called him their country's greatest son. A journalist for the *London Times* rushed off to send a telegram to newspapers all over the world. When the world heard the news about the experiment, people believed Pasteur would relieve the burden of suffering from all mankind. France awarded him the Legion of Honor. Pasteur not only saved his reputation, but approximately 400,000 animals were vaccinated in the following year.

Farmers wrote to Pasteur, begging him for thousands of doses of the anthrax vaccine. Pasteur turned his laboratory into a vaccine factory. Then Roux, Chamberland, and Louis Thuillier, a new assistant, traveled all over France and into Hungary, vaccinating hundreds of sheep and other animals.

Working day and night to provide farmers with enough vaccine, the scientists became totally exhausted, but Pasteur was already thinking of his next challenge. He set out to develop a vaccine for the deadly rabies virus.

London Times

On June 3, 1881, a *London Times* article stated: "Pasteur, one of the scientific glories of France, made to-day experiments . . . on that malady dreaded by agriculturists, called 'charbon' [anthrax], a sickness which rages more especially among sheep, the mortality of which produced by it is estimated in France at several million francs a year."[3]

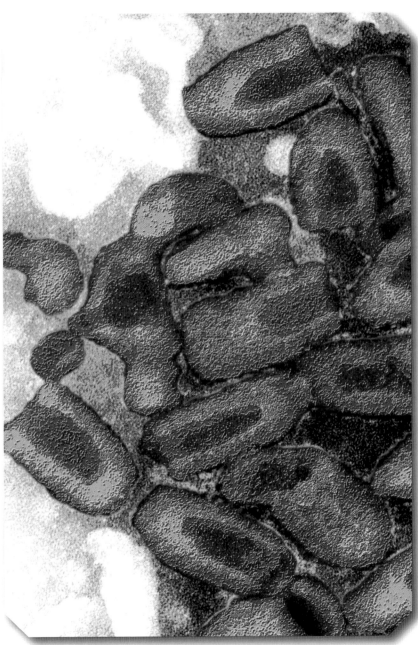

Viewed under a microscope, the rabies virus is recognizable by its bullet shape.

Pasteur used these items to dry rabbit marrow.

Vaccine for Rabies

*I*t had been two years since Pasteur's anthrax vaccine triumph at Pouilly-le-Fort. He had since studied pneumonia in cattle and developed a vaccine for erysipelas, a contagious disease infecting pigs. In 1883, his assistants and other scientists went to Alexandria, Egypt, to battle a human cholera epidemic. His young assistant Louis Thuillier contracted the disease there and died.

Pasteur was growing old; he walked with a limp and tired easily. But he was still passionately studying the multitude of bacteria that caused animals and people to become sick. He still had vivid memories of his three daughters—Jeanne, Camille, and Cécile—who had been taken from him by deadly diseases.

Testing Rabies

In 1884, the 61-year-old Pasteur was deep into the study of rabies—commonly called hydrophobia. His laboratory housed a rabid bulldog with green foam spewing from its mouth. Its growl was low and gravelly, and its eyes rolled continually. At Pasteur's direction, two of his assistants, hands protected by thick gloves, lifted the dog onto a table and held its head still.

With a hollow glass tube in his mouth, Pasteur approached the dog's face. He placed the end of the tube in the green foam and sucked some of it into the tube. Then he drew the saliva into a syringe and injected it into several pigs. All the pigs got rabies.

The test confirmed that rabies was spread through saliva.

Pasteur, Roux, and Chamberland had been studying rabies for five years, but they had not been able to find the organism responsible for the disease. Pasteur believed that rabies attacked the brain and the nervous system. That was where they would look for the germ.

A New Vaccine

Once Pasteur and his assistants confirmed that rabies attacked the spinal cord and brain, they began working to make a vaccine for rabies. Pasteur removed the spinal cord from a rabbit that had died of rabies and hung it inside a large sterile tube to dry. Fourteen days later, using the dried spinal cord, he concocted a solution of weakened rabies from the dried-out spinal cord. He then injected the solution into several healthy dogs. For two weeks, the dogs

Hydrophobia

Rabies is also called hydrophobia. However, the fear of drinking water is only one symptom of rabies. At onset, rabies symptoms are headache, fever, pain, uncontrollable movements, depression, and hydrophobia. A victim eventually experiences hallucinations and falls into a coma. The spread of rabies is controlled primarily by vaccinating dogs.

received a daily injection of the rabies solution. Each remained healthy, which pleased Pasteur. His next step was to inject the dogs with a deadly dose of rabies. None of the dogs developed the disease.

Pasteur then wanted to find out whether the weakened rabies solution would be effective if administered after a dog was bitten. He put two healthy dogs into a cage with a rabid dog. Both dogs were bitten. Over the next 14 days, one of the dogs was injected daily with the rabies vaccine. The vaccinated dog did not get sick; the other dog died of rabies. One month later, Pasteur wrote about the vaccinated dog in his laboratory notebook, "He has not evidenced one symptom of hydrophobia. He is immune. The vaccine is a success."[1]

Vaccine for Humans?

Pasteur was afraid to try his new rabies vaccine on humans. He feared that the vaccine might kill a person, and he would feel like a murderer. Since news of his rabies vaccine had been made public, he had received hundreds of letters. Desperate parents begged him to use his vaccine on their children who had been bitten by rabid animals. Even leaders of other countries asked him when the vaccine could be available for humans. Others cautioned him about the dangers of experimenting with human life. Pasteur finally decided there was only one safe way to test the vaccine on a person. He would allow himself to be bitten by a rabid dog and vaccinate himself. He would tell no one about his plan.

Before Pasteur could put his plan into action, three frantic people from Alsace arrived at his laboratory. One was Theodore Vone, a grown man who had been attacked on the arm by his rabid dog on July 4, 1885. The other two were a mother and her nine-year-old son, Joseph Meister. On Joseph's way to school that same day, he had been attacked and bitten 14 times by the same dog. Joseph's face, arms, hands, and thighs were wrapped in bandages. Fear glazed the eyes of both the boy and his mother. The mother begged Pasteur to help her son.

Pasteur first told Vone that he would be alright, since the dog bites had not broken his skin. But Joseph's wounds were deep and gruesome. He needed treatment. Pasteur did not know whether his vaccine would cure the boy or make his rabies worse. He was not a medical doctor, and it was illegal for him to treat patients. Pasteur asked two medical doctors, Dr. Joseph Grancher and Dr. Alfred

Vulpian, to look at Joseph's wounds. Vulpian, a member of the Rabies Commission, was certain that the boy would die of rabies if he were not treated. Vulpian encouraged Pasteur and told him it was his duty to try the vaccine on Joseph. Grancher agreed with his colleague.

A SERIES OF INJECTIONS

Pasteur immediately called for Roux and Chamberland to prepare a rabies vaccine for Joseph Meister. That evening, Pasteur gave the boy his first injection—a few drops of a rabies solution made from the spinal cord of the

Report to the Academy of Sciences

On October 26, 1885, Pasteur presented his findings on the rabies vaccine to the French Academy of Sciences. He detailed his treatment of Joseph Meister and the start of Jean-Baptiste Jupille's treatment. His report about the Meister boy read in part:

As the death of this child appeared inevitable, I decided, not without deep and severe unease, as one can well imagine, to try on Joseph Meister the procedure which had consistently worked in dogs. . . . on July 6, at 8 in the evening, sixty hours after the bites of July 4 . . . injected under a fold of skin in the right hypochondrium [upper abdomen], one-half . . . syringe of spinal cord of a rabbit dead of rabies on June 21 and conserved since then in a flask of dry air, that is to say for 15 days. . . . [P]erhaps the most serious question to resolve at this moment is the allowable interval between the moment of a bite and when one begins treatment. This interval in the case of Joseph Meister was two and a half days. But it should be expected that this could be much longer.[2]

rabbit. Joseph received a total of 13 injections.
Each day, the rabies solution was stronger. Over
the next two weeks, Joseph's wounds began to heal.
He grew stronger and showed no signs of rabies.
By mid-August, a month after his treatments ended,
Joseph was still healthy. Pasteur concluded that the
vaccine had been successful. Joseph and his mother
returned home.

HOPE FOR THE WORLD

In October, just two months later, 15-year-old
Jean-Baptiste Jupille arrived at Pasteur's laboratory.
It had been seven days since Jean-Baptiste had been
bitten by a rabid dog. But it was not too late to save
him. Pasteur went through the same process of 13
injections. The teenage boy was saved from rabies.

News of the successful rabies treatments raced
throughout the world. Victims of rabid dog attacks
appeared at Pasteur's laboratory from as far away
as Russia and the United States. Four American
children had recently been attacked by rabid dogs.
The *New York Herald* newspaper quickly raised enough
money to send them to Paris for treatment. The
children received the rabies injections and returned
home, healthy and strong.

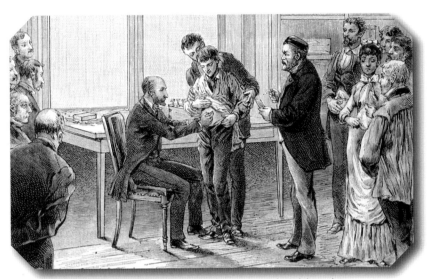

Pasteur watches as a young boy is inoculated for rabies.

Eight months after Pasteur treated Joseph
Meister, approximately 350 people had gone to his
laboratory for treatment. Only a few treatments
failed—those in which too much time had elapsed
since the people had been bitten. Nine-year-old
Louise Pelletier arrived at the laboratory 37 days
after she had been bitten. Pasteur tried to save her,
but the injections were given too late. An emotional
Pasteur was with her when she died in December.
While Pasteur's adversaries tried to use the young
girl's death against him, Louise Pelletier's father
praised Pasteur for his efforts.

A New Laboratory

Scientists and doctors all over Europe flocked to Paris to meet Pasteur. The people of France burst with pride for the man who was saving so many people's lives. In January 1886, donations began flooding in from countries all over the world. The money was for a larger laboratory that could handle more rabies victims. Pasteur received a long list of donors' names. One name especially stood out— Joseph Meister.

What Happened to Joseph Meister?

Joseph Meister, the first human to receive Pasteur's vaccine for rabies, became caretaker of the Pasteur Institute. In 1940, the Nazis occupied Paris and demanded access to the tombs of Louis and Marie Pasteur at the institute. Meister refused, and then, in a state of extreme hopelessness, committed suicide. He was 64.

Construction of the new laboratory in Paris would start in January 1887. Pasteur's colleagues named it the Pasteur Institute. It would treat thousands of rabies victims and be a center of research for studying more of the world's diseases. But it would be more than a center for treatment and research. It would be a tribute and a monument to Louis Pasteur, the scientist who dedicated his life to finding ways to protect animals and people from disease.

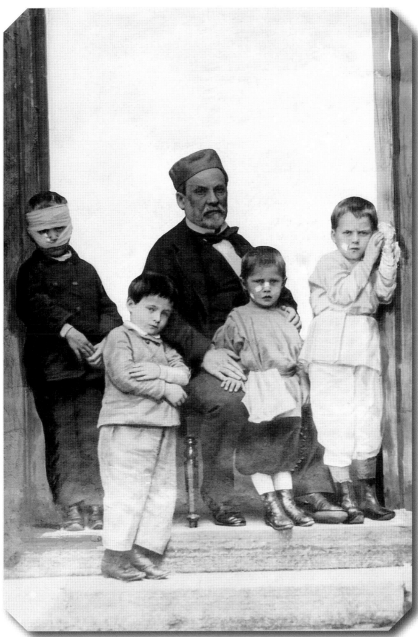

Pasteur treated these children who had been bitten by rabid dogs.

The laboratory of the Pasteur Institute in the early twentieth century

THE PASTEUR INSTITUTE

asteur was 65 years old when the Pasteur Institute was completed in 1888. It was a center for the treatment of rabies and research into other contagious diseases. Pasteur also considered it a place for advanced scientific studies. Appointed the

institute's first director, Pasteur held the position
for the rest of his life. Board members included
not only some of the most notable French scientists
and doctors of the time but successful bankers and
prominent journalists as well.

FESTIVE INAUGURATION

The Pasteur Institute was inaugurated in a festive
occasion on November 14, 1888. The streets bustled
with well-wishers, friends, colleagues, dignitaries,
and mounted police. Musicians provided majestic
music that matched the grand event, and residents
watched from their balconies and rooftops. Special
invitations had been sent to 1,200 people, who were
the only ones allowed inside.

Pasteur arrived at noon, holding onto the arm of
his son, Jean-Baptiste. They walked slowly past the
musicians and up the stairs to the main entrance.
There, Pasteur welcomed ambassadors, foreign
representatives, and scientists from all over the
world. France's heads of state and President Sadi
Carnot were also present.

Inside, numerous speeches were delivered.
Pasteur's speech was to be given last. A year earlier,
on October 23, 1887, he had suffered another

stroke, followed by yet another one a few days later. Now, at the inauguration of the institute named after him, he rose from his seat, weak and tired. Then he turned to his colleagues seated nearby and told them he felt "defeated by time."[1] His speaking abilities had not returned to normal. Pasteur sat down and handed a written copy of his speech to his son.

Jean-Baptiste arose, walked to the podium, and delivered his father's speech. Pasteur's words encouraged research and teaching at the new institute. Pasteur also mentioned that, against his will, his name had been carved above the gates:

> *I continue to object to a title that pays homage to a man rather than to a doctrine. . . . What I am here asking of you, and what you in turn will ask of those whom you will train, is the most difficult thing the inventor has to learn. To believe that one has found an important scientific fact to be consumed by the desire to announce it, and yet to be constrained to combat this impulse for days, weeks, sometimes years, to endeavor to ruin one's own experiments, and to announce one's discovery only after one has laid to rest all the contrary hypotheses, yes, that is indeed an arduous task.[2]*

Pasteur's son continued his father's speech passionately, "But when after all these efforts one finally achieves certainty, one feels one of the deepest joys it is given to the human soul to experience."[3]

ACTIVE MIND

In spite of Pasteur's physical limitations from the strokes, he continued to work. His mind was active, and he was constantly thinking of ways to solve problems related to disease and bacteria. He thought of ways to develop more vaccines and hired some of the top scientists in the world to do research and conduct experiments.

The Pasteur Institute

The Pasteur Institute is famous throughout the world as a center for scientific research for the prevention and treatment of infectious diseases. Located on its original site in Paris, France, the institute employs nearly 2,800 people of more than 60 nationalities, who are involved in research, education, and public health.

Scientists at the institute focus on diseases caused by viruses, which include hepatitis, influenza, AIDS, rabies, and polio. They also study certain types of cancer, genetic diseases, and allergies. Another focus of the institute is educating future scientists. Each year, approximately 250 young scientists from all over the world take upper-level courses in the study of microorganisms and immunity. Each year, more than 800 trainees from 60 countries sharpen their skills in the institute's 130 modern laboratories in its ten research departments.

The Pasteur Institute includes a medical center for public health services. It offers vaccinations and medications for diseases such as hepatitis, diphtheria, tetanus, whooping cough, influenza, tuberculosis, and malaria. The center also regularly treats a variety of infectious and tropical diseases. It houses an active rabies center and a screening center for AIDS and hepatitis C. The institute has 32 other branches on five continents.

The scientists kept Pasteur informed of their work and the progress they were making.

Pasteur worked at the institute as long as he could. He passed on many of his new ideas to younger scientists and emphasized what he had always believed—that science must serve all humanity. Pasteur wanted this to happen within the walls of his magnificent new institute.

In 1892, Pasteur's health declined, and he confined himself to his room. In May, a committee of people from all over the world began planning a special celebration for the aging Pasteur. It would take place on his seventieth birthday at the great Sorbonne University. Four thousand invitations were sent out, and France declared his birthday a national holiday.

FINAL CELEBRATION

On December 27, 1892, scientists, doctors, professors, foreign dignitaries, and students crowded into the Sorbonne auditorium. Even some of Pasteur's old adversaries attended the event. Their resentments and doubts had been replaced with admiration. Dr. Joseph Lister was also present. He was the first doctor to put into practice Pasteur's theory of clean hands and clean hospitals. The sterilization process at Lister's hospital had saved many lives.

Pasteur entered the room on the arm of Sadi Carnot, the fourth president of the French republic. The crowd erupted in thunderous ovation. Pasteur took a seat on the platform. Speeches from kings, presidents, scientists, and doctors praised Pasteur. When Dr. Lister came to the platform, Pasteur stood slowly and embraced him.

When it came time for Pasteur to speak, his son, Jean-Baptiste, once again read the speech his father had written for the occasion. It was directed at the young scientists who were still studying and learning. The words of his father's speech told them not to become discouraged and to ask themselves first, "What have I done to acquire knowledge?"[4] Then ask, "What have I done for my country?"[5]

"But to whatever degree life will have favored your efforts, when you approach the great goal, you must be able to say to yourself: 'I have done my best.'"[6]

—*Louis Pasteur*

Final Years

Over the next few years, Pasteur's health
continued to decline as more strokes wracked his
body. With his health quickly deteriorating, Pasteur
retired to his room on June 13, 1895. His wife,
Marie, his children, and his grandchildren took
turns reading to him and sitting with him around
the clock.

On September 28, 1895, the 72-year-old Louis
Pasteur died. He was honored with a state funeral.
The huge processional made its way through Paris,
beginning at the Pasteur Institute and ending at the
Notre Dame Cathedral where Pasteur was buried.
Later, his body was moved to a tomb at the Pasteur
Institute. His wife, Marie, died September 28, 1910,
exactly 15 years after the death of her husband. She
was entombed next to him at the Pasteur Institute.

Pasteur was one of the most significant scientists
of all time. He taught the world about research,
experimentation, and discovery. He contributed to
the understanding of germ theory and developed the
pasteurization process. In addition, he pioneered
microbiology, sterilization, and immunology. His
greatest achievement, however, was the vaccine. His
vaccines for cholera, anthrax, rabies, and other

Today, a monument in Pasteur's honor stands in Dole, France, his birthplace.

diseases have saved millions of lives throughout the years.

A Legacy

Discovering a vaccination against rabies was just a beginning. Pasteur's ability to identify a problem and believe a solution could be found is carried on by the Pasteur Institute. He understood the value of working with colleagues with their own diverse strengths. As a teacher, he passed his disciplines and processes on to a new generation.

Today, the Pasteur Institute is comprised of researchers, doctors, and scientists who study the same issues from their particular viewpoint. Their findings are shared to work toward common goals. The institute is funded by donations.

Louis Pasteur's ideas and passion live on through those who continue to wage war against diseases that afflict all humanity. Pasteur lives on through those whose lives have been saved by his discoveries. And he lives on through those who have learned from him—one of the great giants of science. ⁓

Finding HIV

In 1983, nearly 100 years after the opening of the Pasteur Institute, two of its French scientists isolated the HIV virus, which causes AIDS. In 2008, the two scientists—Françoise Barré-Sinoussi and Luc Montagnier—were jointly awarded the Nobel Prize in Physiology or Medicine for their discovery.

The Pasteur Institute, or Institut Pasteur in French, in Paris

Timeline

1822	1831	1839
Louis Pasteur is born on December 27 in Dole, France.	Pasteur begins school at the age of eight in Arbois, France.	Pasteur attends the Royal College of Besançon.

1852	1854	1856
Pasteur is promoted to full professor of chemistry at the University of Strasbourg.	Pasteur becomes a professor of chemistry and the dean of science at the University of Lille.	Pasteur begins experiments with fermentation.

1846

While attending the École Normale Supérieure in Paris, Pasteur begins experimenting with crystals.

1848

Pasteur presents his findings on crystals.

1849

Pasteur becomes a professor of chemistry at the University of Strasbourg in France. He marries Marie Laurent on May 29.

1857

Pasteur is appointed assistant director of scientific studies at the École Normale Supérieure.

1859

Pasteur's nine-year-old daughter Jeanne dies of typhoid fever in September.

1864

Pasteur presents the results of his experimentation on spontaneous generation at the Sorbonne in Paris.

TIMELINE

1865

Pasteur identifies the germs that are making France's wines go sour and discovers the pasteurization process.

1865

Pasteur sets up a laboratory in Alès to determine why France's silkworms are dying.

1865

Pasteur's two-year old daughter Camille dies of a liver tumor.

1873

Pasteur is elected to the National Academy of Medicine.

1879–1881

Pasteur develops vaccines for cholera in chickens and anthrax in sheep.

1885

Pasteur completes the testing of a new rabies vaccine and administers it to a human.

1866

Pasteur's 12-year-old daughter Cécile dies of typhoid fever in May.

1868

Construction on a laboratory for Pasteur begins at the École Normale.

1868

Pasteur suffers a stroke on October 19.

1888

The Pasteur Institute in Paris opens.

1892

France celebrates and declares Pasteur's birthday, December 27, a national holiday.

1895

Pasteur dies on September 28 at the age of 72.

ESSENTIAL FACTS

DATE OF BIRTH

December 27, 1822

PLACE OF BIRTH

Dole, France

DATE OF DEATH

September 28, 1895

PARENTS

Jean-Joseph Pasteur and Jeanne-Etiennette Roqui

EDUCATION

Royal College of Besançon; École Normale Supérieure

MARRIAGE

Marie Laurent (May 29, 1849)

CHILDREN

Jeanne, Jean-Baptiste, Cécile, Marie Louise, and Camille

Career Highlights

Pasteur developed a heating process that killed the harmful microorganisms causing food spoilage. The process came to be called pasteurization and is still applied today in the wine, beer, and dairy industries. Pasteur developed vaccines for several infectious diseases, including anthrax, cholera, and rabies. In 1888, Pasteur founded the Pasteur Institute, still one of the most productive scientific research centers in the world.

Societal Contributions

Pasteur is best known for the process of pasteurization to kill organisms in food or beverages that cause diseases. He discovered vaccines that prevent diseases caused by bacteria, including anthrax in cattle and chicken cholera. He also saved the silkworm industry by teaching silkworm cultivators how to examine eggs under a microscope for disease. They kept only disease-free eggs.

Conflicts

There was a controversy among the scientific community regarding the theory of spontaneous generation—the common belief that plants and animals developed from nonliving things. Pasteur's experiments proved the theory of spontaneous generation to be false.

Quote

"Imagination should give wings to our thoughts but we always need decisive experimental proof, and when the moment comes to draw conclusions and to interpret the gathered observations, imagination must be checked and dominated by the factual results of the experiment."—*Louis Pasteur*

Glossary

anthrax
> An infectious, often deadly disease that causes fever, swelling in the throat, and sores on the skin.

bacteria
> One-celled organisms found in all living things; some can cause disease.

carbolic acid
> Chemical compound, also called phenol, used in diluted form as a disinfectant or antiseptic.

chemistry
> Science of the structure, properties, and reactions of chemical elements and compounds.

cholera
> Infectious disease of the small intestine.

comatose
> In a state of unconsciousness.

compound
> Consisting of two or more chemical elements.

crystal
> A solid body with a symmetrical structure.

deflect
> To turn aside or cause to bend.

fermentation
> Chemical reaction in which yeast converts sugar to alcohol.

flask
> Rounded glass container with a narrow neck.

immune
> Protected against a specific disease either by naturally acquired resistance or through vaccination.

infectious
> Capable of causing or transmitting infection.

microbiology
Branch of science that studies microorganisms and their effects on humans and animals.

microorganism
Life form, usually consisting of one cell that can be seen only with a microscope.

molecule
Smallest unit of a substance that retains the chemical properties of that substance.

pasteurization
Heating process that kills harmful microorganisms that can cause spoiling or disease in foods or drinks.

rabies
Disease of the nervous system that is transmitted by the saliva of infected animals and is often fatal.

rector
Principal of certain colleges and universities.

refract
To deflect or redirect light from its straight path.

stroke
Medical condition caused by sudden lack of oxygen to the brain that is usually caused by blockage or breaking of a blood vessel.

typhoid fever
Fatal disease caused by bacteria in contaminated food or water.

vaccine
Weakened or dead virus or bacteria injected to produce immunity to a disease.

virus
Extremely small, disease-causing agent.

yeast
Single-celled fungi that reproduce and cause sugars in fruit juices to ferment; also used to make bread dough rise.

Additional Resources

Selected Bibliography

Debré, Patrice. *Louis Pasteur*. Baltimore, MD: The Johns Hopkins University Press, 2000. Print.

Dolan Jr., Edward F. *Pasteur and the Invisible Giants*. New York: Dodd, 1958. Print.

Geison, Gerald L. *The Private Science of Louis Pasteur*. Princeton, NJ: Princeton University Press, 1995. Print.

Vallery-Radot, Pasteur. *Louis Pasteur: A Great Life in Brief*. New York: Knopf, 1961. Print.

Further Readings

Hansen, Bert. *Picturing Medical Progress from Pasteur to Polio*. New Brunswick, NJ: Rutgers University Press, 2009.

Lassieur, Allison. *Louis Pasteur: Revolutionary Scientist*. New York: Children Press, 2005.

MacDonald, Fiona. *Louis Pasteur: Father of Modern Medicine*. Woodbridge, CT: Blackbirch Press, 2001.

Robbins, Louise E. *Louis Pasteur and the Hidden World of Microbes*. New York: Oxford University Press, 2001.

Web Links

To learn more about Louis Pasteur, visit ABDO Publishing Company online at **www.abdopublishing.com**. Web sites about Pasteur are featured on our Book Links page. These links are routinely monitored and updated to provide the most current information available.

Places to Visit

Birthplace of Louis Pasteur
Rue Louis Pasteur 43
Dole, France 39100
33 3 84722061
03 84 72 20 61
www.musee-pasteur.com/index.php?id=149&L=1
The birthplace of Louis Pasteur is preserved as a monument to one
of the greatest scientists of all time.

Institut Pasteur
25 Rue du Dr-Roux, F-75015
Metro station: Pasteur
Paris, France
33 01 45 68 80 00
en.parisinfo.com/museum-monuments/144/musee-pasteur
Still an active center of scientific research for the prevention and
treatment of diseases, the institute includes a museum, Pasteur's
apartment and laboratory, and the tombs of Pasteur and his wife,
Marie.

**Marian Koshland Science Museum of the National Academy of
Sciences**
Northeast corner of Sixth and E Streets NW
Washington, DC 20001
202-334-1201 or 888-567-4526
www.koshland-science-museum.org/exhib_infectious
The *Infectious Disease: Evolving Challenges to Human Health* exhibit features
displays on emerging diseases, vaccines and human immunity,
global distribution of disease, and more.

SOURCE NOTES

Chapter 1. One of the Greatest

1. Gerald L. Geison. *The Private Science of Louis Pasteur*. Princeton, NJ: Princeton University Press, 1995. Print. 215.

2. Axel Munthe. *The Story of San Michele*. New York: E.P. Dutton, 1929. Web. 26 Mar. 2010.

3. Pasteur, *Cahier 94*, fols. 83–83v. Papiers Pasteur, Bibliothèque Nationale, Paris. In Gerald L. Geison. *The Private Science of Louis Pasteur*. Princeton, NJ: Princeton University Press, 1995. Print. 208–209.

4. Gerald L. Geison. *The Private Science of Louis Pasteur*. Princeton, NJ: Princeton University Press, 1995. Print. 213.

5. Ibid. 217.

6. Pasteur Vallery-Radot. *Louis Pasteur: A Great Life in Brief*. New York: Knopf, 1958. Print. v.

Chapter 2. A Tanner's Son

1. Patrice Debré. *Louis Pasteur*. Baltimore, MD: The Johns Hopkins University Press, 2000. Print. 9.

2. Pasteur Vallery-Radot. *Louis Pasteur: A Great Life in Brief*. New York: Knopf, 1958. Print. 13.

3. Ibid.

4. Patrice Debré. *Louis Pasteur*. Baltimore, MD: The Johns Hopkins University Press, 2000. Print. 12.

5. Pasteur Vallery-Radot. *Louis Pasteur: A Great Life in Brief*. New York: Knopf, 1958. Print. 16–17.

6. Ibid. 25.

7. Rene J. Dubos. *Louis Pasteur: Free Lance of Science*. Boston: Little, 1950. Print. 29–30.

8. Patrice Debré. *Louis Pasteur*. Baltimore, MD: The Johns Hopkins University Press, 2000. Print. 23.

Chapter 3. Marriage and Children

1. Pasteur Vallery-Radot. *Louis Pasteur: A Great Life in Brief*. New York: Knopf, 1958. Print. 37.

2. Ibid. 38.

3. Ibid.

4. Ibid. 39.

5. William B. Sarles. "And Gladly Wolde He Lerne and Gladly Teche." Sept. 1967. *Bacteriological Reviews, American Society for Microbiology*. Web. 8 July 2010.

6. Louis Pasteur. *ThinkExist.com Quotations*. Web. 8 Oct. 2010.

Chapter 4. Fermentation and Bacteria

1. Pasteur Vallery-Radot. *Louis Pasteur: A Great Life in Brief*. New York: Knopf, 1958. Print. 78.

2. Patrice Debré. *Louis Pasteur*. Baltimore, MD: The Johns Hopkins University Press, 2000. Print. 124.

3. Ibid.

4. Aristotle. *Book V. History of Animals*. Book V, Part 1. 343 B.C. Trans. by D'Arcy Wentworth Thompson. Oxford, UK: Clarendon, 1910. Web. 17 May 2010.

5. *The Living Age*. Vol. 280. Boston, MA: The Living Age, 1914. Print. 101.

6. Edward F. Dolan Jr. *Pasteur and the Invisible Giants*. New York: Dodd, 1958. Print. 94.

7. Ibid. 95.

Source Notes Continued

Chapter 5. Saving France's Industries
1. Patrice Debré. *Louis Pasteur*. Baltimore, MD: The Johns
Hopkins University Press, 2000. Print. 124.
2. Ibid.
3. Ibid. 126.
4. Edward F. Dolan Jr. *Pasteur and the Invisible Giants*. New York:
Dodd, 1958. Print. 123.

Chapter 6. The Fight against Germs
1. Edward F. Dolan Jr. *Pasteur and the Invisible Giants*. New York:
Dodd, 1958. Print. 134–135.

Chapter 7. Tackling Contagious Diseases
1. Edward F. Dolan Jr. *Pasteur and the Invisible Giants*. New York:
Dodd, 1958. Print. 156.
2. Ibid. 160.
3. Quoted in "Experiments on Diseased Sheep." *Mercury*.
5 Sept. 1881. Web. 20 May 2010.

Chapter 8. Vaccine for Rabies

1. Edward F. Dolan Jr. *Pasteur and the Invisible Giants*. New York: Dodd, 1958. Print. 190.

2. Louis Pasteur. "Method for Preventing Rabies After a Bite." *Bulletin of the Academy of Medicine*. 27 Oct. 1885. Web. 20 May 2010.

Chapter 9. The Pasteur Institute

1. Patrice Debré. *Louis Pasteur*. Baltimore, MD: The Johns Hopkins University Press, 2000. Print. 471.

2. Ibid. 472.

3. Ibid.

4. Ibid. 493.

5. Ibid.

6. Ibid.

INDEX

ABOUT THE AUTHOR

Sue Vander Hook has been writing books for 20 years. Although her writing career began with several nonfiction books for adults, Vander Hook's main focus is nonfiction books for children and young adults. She especially enjoys writing about historical events and biographies of people who made a difference. Her published works also include a high school curriculum and series on disease, technology, and sports. She lives with her family in Mankato, Minnesota.

PHOTO CREDITS

AP Images, cover, 3, 36; Pixtal Images/Photolibrary , 6; Stevens Frederic/SIPA/AP Images, 13; Michael Short/Photolibrary, 14; Louis Pasteur/Bridgeman Art Library, 17; Time & Life Pictures/ Getty Images, 19, 31, 76, 85, 97 (top); Georges Lopez/ Photolibrary, 25, 98 (top); Sylvain Grandadam/Photolibrary, 26, 96; A. & F. Michler/Photolibrary, 32; Charles O'Rear/Corbis, 43; North Wind/North Wind Picture Archives, 44; SONNET Sylvain/Photolibrary, 48; Bahnmueller/Photolibrary, 51; Apic/ Contributor/Getty Images, 55; The Print Collector/Photolibrary, 56; Hulton Archive/Stringer/Getty Images, 61, 66, 97 (bottom); Silvio Fiore/Photolibrary, 65; Stefano Bianchetti/Corbis, 73; Dr. F.A. Murphy/Getty Images, 75; Bettmann/Corbis, 83, 98 (bottom); Roger Viollet/Getty Images, 86; J-C&D. Pratt/ Photolibrary, 93; Annebicque Bernard/Corbis, 95, 99